NICKISMS II

The Book That Everyone Should Write!

Nick Stanfield

NICKISMS II:
THE BOOK THAT EVERYONE SHOULD WRITE!

© 2017 Nick Stanfield

Published by Adriel Publishing

www.adrielpublishing.com

Edited by Elizabeth Ann Lawless

FIRST EDITION

Printed in the U.S.A.

ISBN: 978-1-892324-46-7

DEDICATION

This book is dedicated to those of you
who have the courage and discipline to
take the appropriate action to
Write Your Own Book.

INTRODUCTION TO NICKISMS II

The original outline of Nickisms II was developed for the author's mother in 1990 to help her create a road map for his guidance when the time came. It served his family well in 1996.

In 1996 Nick Stanfield published his first book entitled NICKISMS: ALL YOU NEED TO KNOW ABOUT MANAGING AN ENTREPRENEURIAL BUSINESS. You will get a few of these Nickisms in the copy below and one of those "isms" laid the need for this additional book.

That "isms" is: "The only things certain in life are: death, taxes and accelerated change."

Accelerated change is the driving force here!

The changes in our world are accelerating at warp speed and it is mind bending. In the 90s we were just learning about the internet, personal computers and other devices, passwords, hacking and cyber crimes.

Today it is impertive that we know the ID Name and Password for multiple devices, bank and credit cards. I think and hope you will find this guide as helpful as I found it in my life.

I will leave you with two quotes that I hope will push you forward in writting your own book. They are:

1. From Gone with the Wind, Scarlett O'Hare says
   "I'll think about that tomorrow!!"

2. From Garth Brooks (song)
   "What if tomorrow never comes??"

TABLE OF CONTENTS

THE BOOK THAT EVERYONE SHOULD WRITE!

"A discussion of topics"

Overview: The outline, by topic categories, is for recording all pertinent facts in one's life in one book. *(Authors note: this could be done on a computer assuming one had a backup plan and your love ones knew where to find it on your computer).*

The following categories have been identified as information needed for an individual to leave a "road map" when he/she is no longer able to express his/her wishes to loved ones. The categories are not all-inclusive and may be changed, or added to, to best suit an individual's own circumstances.

If you have purchased the electronic download version of this information, the purchase of a notebook, paper and index system with adequate sections will put you in business.

NICKISM

"There are three kinds of disipline:
spiritual, physical and mental."

1. Critical Information:

That information first needed to begin to manage the affairs of an individual no longer able to do it themselves.

Where are the keys?

_____

_____

_____

_____

Where is any extra cash, stocks or other valuables hidden in the house or elsewhere?

_____

_____

_____

_____

_____

_____

Who can sign on checking accounts?

_____

_____

_____

_____

_____

_____

_____

Where is the list of passwords required to check various accounts, credit cards, computers and the like?

_____

_____

_____

_____

_____

_____

How do you close out credit card accounts?

_____

_____

_____

_____

_____

_____

_____

_____

_____

_____

_____

_____

_____

_____

_____

NICKISM

"Never deal with a person that will lie to you. Because sooner or later they will lie to themselves and they will truly become lost".

2. Personal Advisors:

Who are they, how do you reach them and what areas do they cover? (Lawyer, Accountant, Financial Planner, Pastor, etc.)

_____

_____

_____

_____

_____

_____

_____

_____

_____

_____

_____

_____

_____

NICKISM

**"The common thread of
all successful people:
They are doers".**

3. Personal Financial Affairs:

This includes Banks, Bankers, Bank Accounts and Lock Boxes. The name of each institution, the contact, their title, an address, a phone number and an email if you have one.

_____

_____

_____

_____

_____

_____

_____

_____

_____

_____

_____

_____

_____

NICKISM

"The acceptable standard of performance should be how well we did against how well we should have done".

4. Insurance:

Policies and where they are.

The name of your insurance agent, location or address and phone number. *NOTE: Often Insurance Companies do not pay out unless a claim is filed.*

_____

_____

_____

_____

_____

_____

_____

_____

_____

_____

_____

_____

NICKISM

"My fear is not of trying and failing but rather not trying and being less than I might have been".

5. Investments:

A complete list of all investments and cost.

_____

_____

_____

_____

_____

_____

_____

_____

_____

_____

_____

_____

_____

_____

_____

Where are the certificates located?

_____

_____

_____

_____

_____

_____

_____

Brokerage accounts and Individual Brokers with location and phone numbers.

_____

_____

_____

_____

_____

_____

_____

_____

_____

_____

_____

_____

_____

_____

_____

If you have any private investments it is important to give a detailed discussion on each one and probably a section on each such investment.

_____

_____

_____

_____

_____

_____

NICKISM

"An individual's equity is to the balance sheet as the foundation is to a building."

6. Real Estate:

A complete list of all real estate and cost.

_____

_____

_____

_____

_____

_____

_____

_____

_____

_____

_____

_____

_____

_____

_____

_____

_____

Where are the deeds?

_____

_____

_____

_____

_____

_____

_____

_____

_____

_____

_____

_____

_____

_____

_____

NICKISM

"We are all on commission no matter the source of our compensation."

7. Social Security Benefits:

Social Security number and description of current benefits.

_____

_____

_____

_____

_____

_____

_____

_____

_____

_____

_____

_____

_____

_____

At death how to notify Social Security Administration and apply for death benefits.

_____

_____

_____

_____

_____

_____

_____

_____

_____

_____

_____

_____

_____

_____

_____

NICKISM

"The right choices are ones which give an individual the optimum chance for a success and happiness."

8. Estate Plan:

Will - where is it (original) and which firm and lawyer drew it up?

_____

_____

_____

_____

_____

_____

How is probate going to be handled and by whom?

_____

_____

_____

_____

_____

_____

Trust, if any, and who is the trustee?

_____

_____

_____

_____

_____

_____

_____

NICKISM

"Recognition and flexibility are the keys to the successful management of anything."

9. Twelve Month Date Tickler:

By month and date when bills are due.

_____

_____

_____

_____

_____

_____

_____

_____

_____

_____

_____

_____

_____

_____

_____

_____

Some will continue and others must be closed out.

_____

_____

_____

_____

_____

_____

_____

_____

_____

_____

_____

_____

_____

_____

NICKISM

"Always be hungry – always run scared."

10. Inventories:

A detailed inventory, including pictures and appraisals, of all personal and household items. *Note: This is also good to have in case of fire or theft.*

_____

_____

_____

_____

_____

_____

_____

_____

_____

_____

_____

_____

_____

NICKISM

"There is no right way to do a
wrong thing."

11. Family & Friends Information:

Names, addresses, phone numbers and relationship to family members, church, boss, co-workers, and other friends. (An address book can be used for this but it might be helpful to secure a separate copy with this book.)

Who needs to be told about your death?

_____

_____

_____

_____

_____

_____

_____

_____

_____

_____

_____

NICKISM

"Life is about high moral values,
honest, integrity and ethics."

12. Miscellaneous Personal Information & Data:

Personal wishes that may not be covered in your will.

_____

_____

_____

_____

_____

_____

_____

_____

_____

_____

_____

_____

_____

_____

_____

_____

_____

_____

_____

_____

_____

_____

_____

_____

_____

_____

_____

_____

_____

This is not meant to be a legal document and/or replace your will. However, some personal wishes do not seem to make it into one's will. (Ex. Personal items that you wish to leave to friends, loyal employees, care givers or others.)

Conclusion

This is a brief outline, but will allow you to start putting together your own book long before you may feel the time is critical.

But let me remind you we do not all get "six months notice" on when this information may be vital in the efficient and proper management of your personal affairs.

Remember, "what if tomorrow never comes."??

Feel free to expand the topic caterories. For example, you might want to do a section or a whole book on a company or business that you own and manage.

RECOMMENDED READS

The following books are recommended by Stanfield for your reading pleasure and benefit:

1. NICKISMS: ALL YOU NEED TO KNOW ABOUT MANAGING AN ENTREPRENEURIAL BUSINESS
By: Nick Stanfield c1996

2. WHO MOVED MY CHEESE?
By: Spencer Johnson, M.D. c1998

3. ESSENTIALISM: THE DISCIPLINED PURSUIT OF LESS
By: Greg McKeown   c2014

4. THE POWER OF HABIT
By: Charles Duhigg c2012

ABOUT THE AUTHOR

Nick Stanfield is the Founder, President and CEO of MSI Capital Corporation, a Dallas-based investment banking firm specializing in financial management, corporate finance and investment banking services to private entrepreneurial companies. MSI Capital was organized in 1976 and operated until 2016.

Stanfield has been the founder or co-founder of seven operating companies and has invested in another nineteen private companies. MSI Capital has assisted clients secure outside funding of over $100 million since 1976.

MSI Capital has provided financial management services to clients ranging in size from start-up to $50 million in annual revenues.

Stanfield is a graduate of the University of North Texas (BBA-1963), Denton, Texas. He served in banking for six years as an Investment and Trust Officer and with regional investment banking firms as a Vice President for seven years before founding MSI Capital Corporation.

Stanfield is available to speak on this or other entreprenuerial and financial subjects, he can be reached via email: nicks6668@gmail.com or by phone at: 214-415-9223.

Note: if you would like to order multiple copies of the download (pdf) or the paperback version of this book for your organization, please contact me for quantity discounts.

NOTES

NOTES

NOTES

NOTES

NOTES

NOTES